Kathy Brown

Strip-Smart Quilts II

Make 16 Triangle Quilts with One Easy Technique

Martingale
Create with Confidence

Strip-Smart Quilts II: Make 16 Triangle Quilts
with One Easy Technique
© 2013 by Kathy Brown

Martingale®
19021 120th Ave. NE, Ste. 102
Bothell, WA 98011-9511 USA
ShopMartingale.com

Printed in China
18 17 16 15 14 13   8 7 6 5 4 3 2 1

**Library of Congress Cataloging-in-Publication Data
is available upon request.**

ISBN: 978-1-60468-233-5

Mission Statement
Dedicated to providing quality products and
service to inspire creativity.

Credits
President and CEO: Tom Wierzbicki
Editor in Chief: Mary V. Green
Design Director: Paula Schlosser
Managing Editor: Karen Costello Soltys
Acquisitions Editor: Karen M. Burns
Technical Editor: Laurie Baker
Copy Editor: Melissa Bryan
Production Manager: Regina Girard
Cover and Interior Designer: Regina Girard
Photographer: Brent Kane
Illustrator: Lisa Lauch

Contents

Introduction

What began three years ago as a plan to use a simple ruler—the Creative Grids 90° Double-Strip ruler—to make fun and interesting quilts has transformed my quilting journey in ways I never could have imagined. Who would have thought that a single shape—a simple triangle—created from strips sewn together in varying combinations could result in quilts so fun and easy to make, everybody would want to make them? Who would have thought that I'd be teaching classes to masses of quilters across the United States and feeling as though I've only just begun to spread the fun? Certainly not me! You see, I knew when I wrote *Strip-Smart Quilts* (Martingale, 2011) that you could take one ruler—one shape—and use it to create an infinite variety of quilts. Yet I never imagined that quilters worldwide would embrace this concept as I have and be as enthusiastic about creating these quilts as I am. But they are. And they asked for more. And so here we are, with *Strip-Smart Quilts II!*

In these pages are 16 brand-new and exciting designs using the Creative Grids 90° Double-Strip ruler—with some twists! You'll find the familiar combinations of two 2½"-wide strips and four 1½"-wide strips, but in this book I've also added a 4½"-wide strip to the mix, which has infused the quilts with a fresh appeal and even more versatility. Check out how the solid triangles from black 4½"-wide strips are transformed into the night sky behind the mountains in "Evening in Vail" (page 17). Or how the white solid triangles make a blank canvas for the colorful "Kissy Fishy" (page 59). And I didn't stop there! In several of the quilts, such as "Blueberry Pie" (page 21) and "Just Beachy" (page 25), I've added simple squares or strip-set segments between the strip-smart triangles to give the quilts a more airy, modern touch.

But did I stop there? Heavens, no! In taking a look at some of my favorite quilt blocks, I realized that they could be brought to life in new and exciting ways by incorporating strip-smart triangles into their construction. Just take a peek at "Calm before the Storm" (page 51) or "Crow's Feet" (page 75). Simple blocks look stunning with the addition of strip-smart triangles!

So, if you loved the projects in *Strip-Smart Quilts,* I'm sure you're going to embrace these new quilts with just as much fun and enthusiasm as I have. If you haven't yet ventured into strip-smart quilting, now's your chance. Just grab your ruler and a stash of fabrics, and start quilting the strip-smart way! Who knows where your journey may lead you. As for me, I'm on a journey of my own—one that's sure to involve creating even more exciting new strip-smart quilts!

Quiltmaking Basics

Successful strip-smart quilts require a few basic supplies and simple instructions. Follow the guidelines in this section as you construct your quilts.

Materials

- Quilt-shop fabrics
- Thread in a neutral color
- Rotary cutter
- 24" x 36", or larger, cutting mat
- Creative Grids 90° Double-Strip ruler (CGRDBS90)
- 6" square ruler
- Pins
- Seam ripper
- Sewing machine in good working order with a ¼" presser foot
- Spray starch

Rotary Cutting

Because the topic of rotary cutting is covered in so many quilting books, I won't go into great detail here on how to use a rotary cutter. What I do want to emphasize, however, is the importance of beginning each project in this book with a new rotary-cutter blade. You'll be cutting through the seams of strip sets and will need the accuracy that the sharp edge of a new blade provides.

Starch for Success

The quilts in this book use a variety of precut fabrics and yardage found in quilt shops to make strip sets from which triangles are cut using the 90° Double-Strip ruler. Before rotary cutting the triangles, I advise starching the fabric yardage to stabilize it. The cuts you make with the ruler produce bias edges and the starch helps prevent these edges from stretching. If the quilts require precut 2½"-wide strips, which typically come from Jelly Rolls, it's not necessary to starch those strips prior to sewing. But do press your strip sets after sewing them. Press the strips carefully so they remain straight, and don't stretch the strip sets out of shape by twisting and turning the iron. A simple up-and-down, side-to-side pressing motion will ensure straight strip sets.

Cutting Triangles

The blocks for the quilts in this book will include pieces cut from individual strips or strip sets that measure 4½" wide. These include strip sets made from two 2½"-wide strips and strip sets made from four 1½"-wide strips.

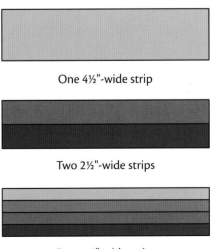

One 4½"-wide strip

Two 2½"-wide strips

Four 1½"-wide strips

Once your strip sets are made, you'll rotary cut triangles from them using the 90° Double-Strip ruler. This ruler makes the cutting process simple, fast, and accurate. Follow the guidelines below for left-hand or right-hand cutting; the basics for ruler placement remain the same.

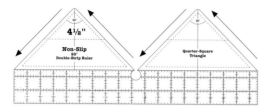

Right-hand cutting follows the ruler from right to left.

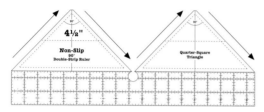

Left-hand cutting follows the ruler from left to right.

1. Lay your strip ruler over a strip set that is right side up, with the left edge of the ruler approximately 1" to the right of the beginning of the strip set, the bottom edge of the triangles on the ruler aligned with the bottom edge of the strip set, and the middle dashed line on the ruler aligned with the middle seam line of the strip set. If you're cutting triangles from an unpieced 4½"-wide strip, just align the bottom edges of the triangles on the ruler and the strip.

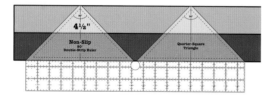

2. Cut your first set of triangles—three in all. The remainder of your strip set will look something like that shown below. Proceed to the next step.

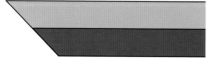

Remainder

3. Rotate the remainder of the strip set 180° so that the fabric strip that was along the top is now along the bottom. Once again, lay your strip ruler down on top of the strip set, this time lining up the *right* sloping edge of the ruler with the cut angle of the strip set, the bottom edge of the triangles on the ruler with the bottom edge of the strip set, and the middle dashed seam line on the ruler with the middle seam line of the strip set. Cut out a second set of three triangles.

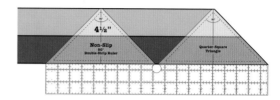

Shown below are the triangle shapes that will result from cutting a 4½"-wide strip, as well as strip sets made from 2½"- and 1½"-wide strips.

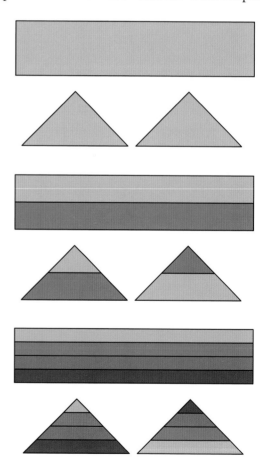

Sub-Cutting Triangles

For one of the quilts in this book, you'll need to cut the triangles created with the 90° Double-Strip ruler in half to make pairs of smaller, mirror-image 90° triangles.

1. Cut triangles as described in "Cutting Triangles" on page 7.
2. Lay a 90° triangle face up on your cutting mat. Place a 6" square ruler on the triangle, lining up the bottom edge of the ruler with the bottom raw edge of the triangle, and aligning the right edge of the ruler with the top of the triangle.

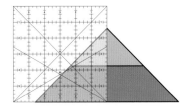

3. Using a rotary cutter, cut the triangle along the right edge of the ruler. The result is two mirror-image 90° triangles.

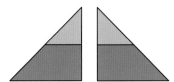

Pinning

To pin or not to pin is an issue that most quilters face in their quilting journey. I've found through much trial and error and angst that it is far better *for me* to take the time and pin my blocks together to get accurate intersecting points, rather than ripping the blocks apart later when they don't mesh. If perfectly matching seams aren't important to you—that is, if they can be slightly "off" and the resulting look isn't a problem for you—then by all means don't take the time to pin!

Pressing

Which direction to press the seam allowances on your strip sets is always a consideration. I generally press toward the darker fabric to avoid color showing through the front, which that can occur if you press toward a lighter fabric.

Happily, for many of the quilts in this book, the seam allowances naturally mesh when you join triangle to triangle. When solid or neutral blocks have been added between the pieced triangle blocks, there aren't any seams to match, so it isn't a concern.

With "Blueberry Pie" (page 21), however, the seam allowances will "collide" when you sew like triangles together. When this occurs, try this method for pinning the triangles: With right sides together, poke a pin through both triangles exactly at the seam lines. Don't push the pin up and back through the layers, as you would if you were pinning the pieces together to sew. Instead, keep the alignment pin pushed straight through the seam lines and use additional pins to pin through all the layers ⅛" to the left and ⅛" to the right of the alignment pin. Then remove the alignment pin. Sew the seam slowly, making sure the seam allowances stay flat and smooth.

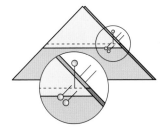

After joining the triangles, press the seam allowances to one side. You'll find that they lie surprisingly flat.

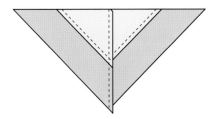

Adding Borders

Many of the quilts in this book don't have borders, but when borders are included, they are constructed with butting corners. Cut the border strips across the width of the fabric and piece them as follows to achieve the length needed.

1. Overlap the strips at right angles, with right sides together. Sew diagonally from corner to corner. Trim the excess fabric, leaving a ¼" seam allowance; press the seam allowances open.

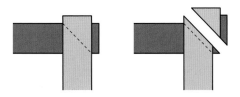

2. Mark the center point on each edge of the quilt top. Mark the center point on one long edge of each border strip. With right sides together, pin the right and left border strips to the quilt top, matching the center points. Note that there will be excess border fabric extending beyond the quilt-top edges. Stitch the borders, and then trim the excess fabric even with the upper and lower edges of the quilt top. Press the seam allowances toward the border strips. Repeat for the top and bottom borders, trimming the excess even with the sides of the quilt top.

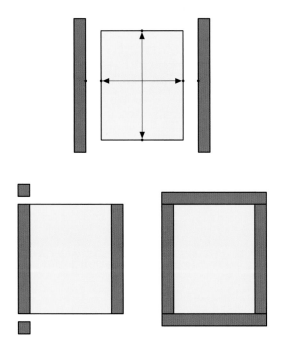

Completing the Quilt

Quilting and binding your quilt are the final steps in the process.

Layering and Quilting

All of the quilts in this book were quilted on long-arm quilting machines, but you can certainly use any quilting method that you prefer. Before the quilting begins, make sure your backing and batting are at least 4" wider and longer than the quilt top. The yardage requirements in each project have allowed for these extra inches. Layer the batting between the backing (right side down) and the quilt top (right side up), baste the layers together, and then quilt as desired.

Binding

Each quilt includes yardage sufficient to cut 2½"-wide binding strips across the width of the fabric.

1. Join the strips with a diagonal seam and trim, leaving a ¼" seam allowance. Press the seam allowances open so that the binding will lie flat when stitched to the quilt. Press the strip in half lengthwise, wrong sides together.

2. Leaving an 8" tail at the beginning, sew the binding to the quilt top using a ¼" seam allowance. Miter the corners as shown.

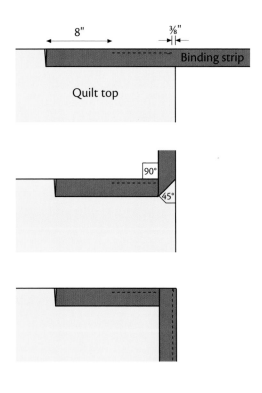

3. Stop sewing when you're about 12" from the beginning; backstitch. Lay the end of the strip over the beginning of the strip, and trim the ends of the strips so they overlap by 2½" (or the width of your binding strips). Sew the ends together as shown and trim, leaving a ¼" seam allowance. Press the seam allowances open. Reposition the binding on the quilt and finish sewing.

Overlapped ends

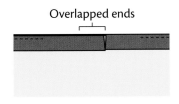

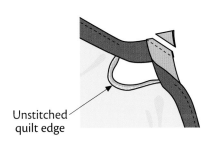

Unstitched quilt edge

4. Fold the edge of the binding to the back of the quilt and hand stitch it down, mitering the corners. I find that the binding folds over the edge more easily if I starch and press it toward the sewn edge.

Quilt back

Streak of Lightning

In southern Louisiana we can experience heavy thunderstorms in the summer months, not to mention the hurricanes that visit us from time to time. One day during a torrential downpour, the lid of our garbage can blew down the street. My normally logical dad, an engineer, decided he had to retrieve the lid in the middle of the thunderstorm! Armed with his trusty golf umbrella, he set off in the pouring rain, thunder, and—yes—lightning to get the trash-can lid. When he didn't return after a few minutes, my younger brother and I began to worry. After a half hour had passed, we set out to find him. Fortunately, he was just a few houses away, making his way back to us, soaking wet and teetering a bit as he walked. It turns out, lightning had struck nearby and the force had knocked our dad to the ground, rendering him immobile for several minutes. He made it home to safety, minus the umbrella, but with his health intact—and with the prized garbage-can lid in his possession.

The bold yellow-and-white chevron pattern that forms in the construction of this quilt reminded me instantly of that day long ago, and the streak of lightning that I'll never forget!

Materials

Yardage is based on 42"-wide fabric.

3⅝ yards of white tone-on-tone fabric for blocks and binding

3⅛ yards of bright yellow tone-on-tone fabric for blocks

3⅞ yards of fabric for backing

63" x 74" piece of batting

Cutting

From the bright yellow tone-on-tone fabric, cut:
- 40 strips, 2½" x 42"

From the white tone-on-tone fabric, cut:
- 47 strips, 2½" x 42"

Constructing the Blocks

1. With right sides together, sew a white strip to a bright yellow strip. Repeat to make a total of 40 strip sets. Open and starch each strip set as described in "Starch for Success" on page 7.

Make 40.

2. Referring to "Cutting Triangles" on page 7, cut six 90° double-strip triangles from each strip set.

3. Separate the triangles into two sets:
   - 120 white tip/yellow strip
   - 120 yellow tip/white strip

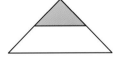

Make 120 of each.

4. With right sides together, sew a white tip/yellow strip triangle to a yellow tip/white strip triangle. Repeat to make a total of 120 blocks. Starch each block to preserve the bias edges of the triangles.

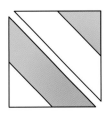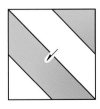

Make 120.

Designed by Kathy Brown; pieced by Linda Reed; quilted by Carol Hilton

Assembling the Quilt Top

1. Using a design wall or other flat surface, arrange the completed blocks into rows 1 and 2 as shown, orienting the blocks in row 1 with the white tip in the upper-left corner and orienting the blocks in row 2 with the white tip in the lower-left corner. Make six of each row.

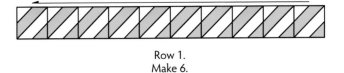

Row 1.
Make 6.

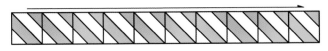

Row 2.
Make 6.

2. Referring to the quilt assembly diagram below, sew the rows together to form the quilt top. Press the seam allowances in one direction.

Finishing

Refer to "Completing the Quilt" on page 10 as needed.

1. Layer the quilt top with batting and backing. Baste the layers, and then quilt as desired.
2. Sew the remaining white 2½" x 42" strips together to make one long strip, and use the strip to bind the quilt.

Quilt assembly

Evening in Vail

Finished quilt: 44½" x 60½"

For much of my adult life I worked in the petrochemical industry as a senior designer, and for a number of those years I managed a computer-aided design drafting system. Training on that system took me to Denver, Colorado, and the beautiful Rocky Mountains. For a girl from southern Louisiana, each venture to Denver brought new and delightful experiences during the different seasons of the year. During one memorable trip, I traveled to Vail on a lazy late-September afternoon. The stunning image of the mountains aglow as afternoon turned into evening, with the aspen trees just beginning to change color, was a sight I'll never forget.

When I found the fabrics for this quilt, they instantly brought a mental picture of that trip to Vail, and I wanted to capture that memory in a meaningful way. Set against a black background, I think these "mountains" accomplished that task.

Materials

Yardage is based on 42"-wide fabric.

2 yards of black solid for background

⅝ yard of very light brownish-green batik for blocks and binding

⅝ yard of light brownish-green batik for blocks and binding

1 yard of medium brownish-green batik for blocks, border, and binding

⅝ yard of dark brownish-green batik for blocks and binding

3 yards of fabric for backing

52" x 68" piece of batting

Cutting

From *each* of the 4 values of brownish-green batiks, cut:

- 8 strips, 1½" x 42" (32 total)
- 2 strips, 2½" x 42" (8 total)

From the black solid, cut:

- 10 strips, 2½" x 42"
- 9 strips, 4½" x 42"

From the remainder of the medium brownish-green batik, cut:

- 6 strips, 2½" x 42"

Constructing the Blocks

1. With right sides together, join one each of the very light, light, medium, and dark batik 1½" x 42" strips in gradating order of value to make a strip set. Repeat to make a total of eight strip sets. Open and starch each strip set as described in "Starch for Success" on page 7.

Make 8.

2. Referring to "Cutting Triangles" on page 7, cut six 90° multi-strip triangles from each strip set and six solid triangles from each black 4½" x 42" strip. Starch each black triangle to preserve the bias edges.

3. Separate the triangles into three sets:
   - 24 light tip/dark strip
   - 24 dark tip/light strip
   - 54 black solid

Make 24.   Make 24.   Make 54.

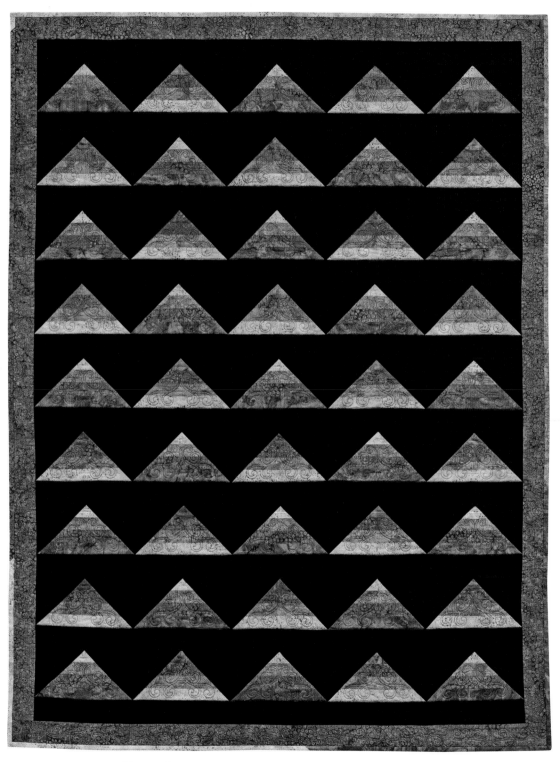

Designed by Kathy Brown; pieced by Linda Reed; quilted by Carol Hilton

Making the Rows

1. Sew six black triangles, three triangles with light tips, and two triangles with dark tips together as shown to make row 1. Starch the pieces again after you add each black triangle to preserve the bias edges. Repeat to make five of row 1.

Row 1.
Make 5.

2. Sew six black triangles, three triangles with dark tips, and two triangles with light tips together as shown to make row 2, again starching after adding each black triangle. Repeat to make four of row 2.

Row 2.
Make 4.

3. Trim the black triangles at the end of each row ¼" from the lower point.

¼"

Assembling the Quilt Top

1. Using a design wall or other flat surface, arrange the completed rows as shown in the quilt assembly diagram at right.
2. Refer to "Adding Borders" on page 10 and the assembly diagram to sew the rows together, adding a black 2½" x 42" sashing strip between each row and at the top and bottom of the joined rows; press the seam allowances toward the sashing strips, and then trim the sashing strips even with the sides of the block rows.

3. Refer to "Adding Borders" to sew medium batik 2½" x 42" strips to the top and bottom of the quilt top; trim and press. Join two medium batik 2½" x 42" border strips to make one long strip. Repeat to make a second pieced strip. Sew these strips to the sides of the quilt top; trim and press.

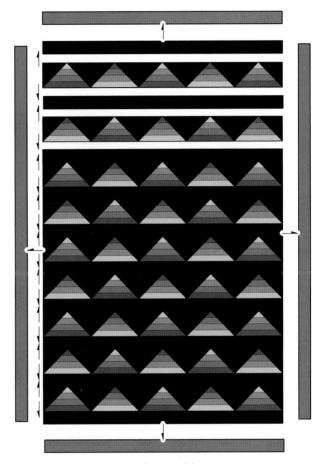

Quilt assembly

Finishing

Refer to "Completing the Quilt" on page 10 as needed.

1. Layer the quilt top with batting and backing. Baste the layers, and then quilt as desired.
2. Sew the remaining batik 2½" x 42" strips together randomly to make one long strip, and use the strip to bind the quilt.

Blueberry Pie

I have always loved sweets. From a bit of chocolate to a slice of cheesecake and everything in between—if it's sweet, it will find its way into my heart! In my younger years, a favorite dessert was my mom's blueberry pie. My dad and I would enjoy it straight out of the oven with a scoop of creamy vanilla ice cream on top. Nothing could have been better! Sometimes I'd scoop out all of the gooey blueberry insides, eating them first and saving for last the flaky crust, swimming in the melted pool of vanilla ice cream! Lips and teeth momentarily stained purple, Dad and I would share a quiet laugh at each other and enjoy the fruits of Mom's labor.

Memories like this that I shared with my dad tend to find their way into my quilts, as they did here in "Blueberry Pie." From the Blueberry blocks to the Crust blocks to the Ice Cream-and-Pie blocks themselves, this quilt will be a favorite of mine for all time!

Materials
Yardage is based on 42"-wide fabric.
4⅛ yards of cream tone-on-tone fabric for blocks
15 assorted blue tone-on-tone 2½" x 42" strips for blocks and binding
15 assorted brown tone-on-tone 2½" x 42" strips for blocks and binding
4 yards of fabric for backing
64" x 80" piece of batting

Cutting
From the cream tone-on-tone fabric, cut:
- 26 strips, 2½" x 42"
- 8 strips, 8½" x 42"; crosscut into 32 squares, 8½" x 8½"

Constructing the Blocks
1. With right sides together, sew a cream strip to a blue strip. Repeat to make a total of 11 blue strip sets. Sew a cream strip to a brown strip. Repeat to make a total of 11 brown strip sets.

Open and starch each strip set as described in "Starch for Success" on page 7. Set aside the remaining blue and brown strips for the binding.

Make 11.

Make 11.

2. Referring to "Cutting Triangles" on page 7, cut six 90° double-strip triangles from each strip set.

Designed by Kathy Brown; pieced by Linda Reed; quilted by Carol Hilton

3. Separate the triangles into four sets. (**Note:** You'll have one each of the cream tip/blue strip, blue tip/cream strip, and brown tip/ cream strip triangles left over, and five of the cream tip/brown strip triangles left over.)

- 33 cream tip/blue strip
- 33 blue tip/cream strip
- 33 cream tip/brown strip
- 33 brown tip/cream strip

Make 33 of each.

4. With right sides together, join four assorted cream tip/blue strip triangles as shown. Repeat to make a total of eight Blueberry blocks.

Blueberry Pie block.
Make 8.

5. Repeat step 4 to make seven Crust blocks using four assorted cream tip/brown strip triangles and 16 Ice Cream-and-Pie blocks using two assorted blue tip/cream strip triangles and two assorted brown tip/cream strip triangles.

Crust block.
Make 7.

Ice Cream-and-Pie block.
Make 16.

Assembling the Quilt Top

1. Using a design wall or other flat surface, arrange the completed blocks as shown in the quilt assembly diagram below. Sew the rows together to form the quilt top; press.

2. Referring to "Adding Borders" on page 10, join two cream 2½" x 42" strips to make one long strip. Repeat to make a second pieced strip. Sew the strips to the top and bottom of the quilt top for the border; press and trim.

Quilt assembly

Finishing

Refer to "Completing the Quilt" on page 10 as needed.

1. Layer the quilt top with batting and backing. Baste the layers, and then quilt as desired.

2. Sew the remaining blue and brown 2½" x 42" strips together randomly to make one long strip, and use the strip to bind the quilt.

Just Beachy

Aaaah, summertime and trips to the beach! Sugar-white sand, crystal-clear blue water, and long walks at sunset all make for the perfect vacation in my opinion. One of my favorite things to see on my walks is all of the colorful beach umbrellas. Whether looking down on them from a high-rise hotel room or passing them at eye level on the beach, I find they provide a welcome respite from the hot summer sun and glare of the shore. When I came upon this group of colorful fabrics, those beach umbrellas instantly came to mind, and I knew this quilt was begging to be made! Grab a stack of colorful strips and whip up your own version of this ever-so-easy beach quilt.

Materials

Yardage is based on 42"-wide fabric.

4½ yards of white tone-on-tone fabric for blocks, filler pieces, sashing, and border

½ yard *each* of pink, blue, yellow, and green swirl prints for blocks and binding

4¼ yards of fabric for backing

68" x 78" piece of batting

Air-soluble pen

Cutting

From *each* of the pink, blue, yellow, and green swirl prints, cut:

- 6 strips, 1½" x 42" (24 total)
- 2 strips, 2½" x 42" (8 total)

From the white tone-on-tone fabric, cut:

- 10 strips, 6" x 42"; crosscut into:
  8 rectangles, 6" x 8¾"
  23 rectangles, 6" x 11½"
- 6 strips, 4½" x 42"
- 24 strips, 2½" x 42"

Constructing the Blocks

1. With right sides together, join one each of the pink, blue, yellow, and green 1½" x 42" strips as shown to make a strip set. Repeat to make a total of six strip sets. Open and starch each strip set as described in "Starch for Success" on page 7.

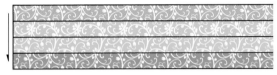

Make 6.

2. Referring to "Cutting Triangles" on page 7, cut six 90° multi-strip triangles from each strip set and six solid triangles from each white tone-on-tone 4½" x 42" strip. Starch each white triangle to preserve the bias edges.

3. Separate the triangles into three sets. (**Note:** You'll have four pink tip/green strip triangles and four white solid triangles left over.)
   - 14 pink tip/green strip
   - 18 green tip/pink strip
   - 32 white solid

Make 14.   Make 18.   Make 32.

Designed by Kathy Brown; pieced by Linda Reed; quilted by Carol Hilton

4. With right sides together, sew a white triangle to each pieced triangle. Starch each block to preserve the bias edges of the triangles.

Make 14. Make 18.

5. Use the air-soluble pen to draw a diagonal line on the white half of each block, marking from the tip of the 90° corner to the center of the long side. Using dark thread, stitch on each drawn line with a straight or satin stitch.

Assembling the Quilt Top

1. Using a design wall or other flat surface, arrange the completed blocks and white 6" x 8¾" and 6" x 11½" rectangles as shown in the quilt assembly diagram below. Sew the blocks and rectangles in each row together.

2. Referring to "Adding Borders" on page 10, join two white 2½" x 42" strips to make one long strip. Repeat to make a total of 12 pieced strips for the sashing and borders. Refer to the assembly diagram to sew eight of the pieced strips and the block rows together to form the quilt top; press the seam allowances toward the sashing strips and then trim the sashing even with the quilt sides.

3. Referring to "Adding Borders," sew two of the pieced strips from step 2 to the sides of the quilt top; press and trim. Repeat to add the remaining pieced strips to the top and bottom of the quilt top; press and trim.

Finishing

Refer to "Completing the Quilt" on page 10 as needed.

1. Layer the quilt top with batting and backing. Baste the layers, and then quilt as desired.

2. Sew the pink, blue, yellow, and green 2½" x 42" strips together randomly to make one long strip, and use the strip to bind the quilt.

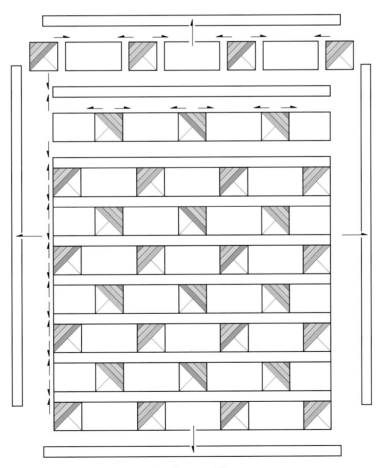

Quilt assembly

Rocky Road

Finished quilt: 40½" x 56½" ➤ **Finished block:** 4" x 4"

 One of my favorite ice cream flavors of all time is rocky road. Decadent chocolate laced with marshmallows, nuts, and dark chocolate chunks is a mouthful of pure pleasure. When I found this array of beautiful black, brown, and cream-colored prints, I knew they were destined for a rocky road quilt. And what a decadent, delightful concoction it turned out to be!

Materials

Yardage is based on 42"-wide fabric.

24 assorted cream tone-on-tone 2½" x 42" strips for blocks

15 assorted dark-brown print 2½" x 42" strips for blocks and binding

15 assorted medium-brown print 2½" x 42" strips for blocks and binding

3 yards of fabric for backing

48" x 64" piece of batting

Constructing the Blocks

1. With right sides together, sew a cream strip to each of 12 assorted dark-brown strips to make 12 strip sets. Repeat to sew a cream strip to each of 12 assorted medium-brown strips to make 12 strip sets. Open and starch each strip set as described in "Starch for Success" on page 7. Set aside the remaining dark-brown and medium-brown strips for the binding.

Make 12.

Make 12.

2. Referring to "Cutting Triangles" on page 7, cut six 90° double-strip triangles from each strip set. Cut each triangle in half to make two smaller, mirror-image triangles as instructed in "Sub-Cutting Triangles" on page 9.

3. Separate the triangles into eight sets:
   - 36 cream tip/dark-brown strip pointing left
   - 36 cream tip/dark-brown strip pointing right
   - 36 dark-brown tip/cream strip pointing left
   - 36 dark-brown tip/cream strip pointing right
   - 36 cream tip/medium-brown strip pointing left
   - 36 cream tip/medium-brown strip pointing right
   - 36 medium-brown tip/cream strip pointing left
   - 36 medium-brown tip/cream strip pointing right

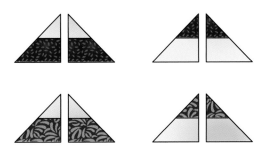

Make 36 of each.

4. With right sides together, sew a cream tip/dark-brown strip pointing right triangle to a cream tip/dark-brown strip pointing left triangle as shown; press. Repeat to make a total of 36 blocks. Sew the remaining

Designed by Kathy Brown; pieced by Linda Reed; quilted by Carol Hilton

triangles together in the same manner to make the number of blocks indicated of each color combination. (**Note:** You'll have a total of eight triangles left over.) Starch each block to preserve the bias edges of the triangles.

Make 36.

Make 35.

Make 34.

Make 35.

Assembling the Quilt Top

1. Using a design wall or other flat surface, arrange the completed blocks as shown in the quilt assembly diagram below.
2. Sew the blocks in each row together; press. Sew the rows together to complete the quilt top. Press the seam allowances in one direction.

Finishing

Refer to "Completing the Quilt" on page 10 as needed.

1. Layer the quilt top with batting and backing. Baste the layers, and then quilt as desired.
2. Sew the remaining brown 2½" x 42" strips together randomly to make one long strip, and use the strip to bind the quilt.

Quilt assembly

Dinosaur Tracks

When our daughter was four and in love with dinosaurs like every other child that age, we had the opportunity to visit a large exhibition in New Orleans that featured animatronic dinosaurs. Her experience with dinosaurs up to that point had been largely through popular children's movies and television shows. Friendly, smiling creatures in pink and purple, blue and green contrasted sharply with the enormous, lifelike dinosaurs she encountered that day. I still vividly remember her placing her little foot next to the gargantuan foot of the Tyrannosaurus rex and loudly exclaiming that T. rex would never be able to find a pair of shoes to fit his feet!

What a wonderful quilt this would have been to commemorate her first foray into the world of dinosaurs. Perhaps you know of a young child who would love his or her own version of "Dinosaur Tracks."

Materials
Yardage is based on 42"-wide fabric.

3 yards of white solid for blocks

1 yard of blue tone-on-tone fabric for blocks and binding

1 yard of green tone-on-tone fabric for blocks and binding

3½ yards of fabric for backing

58" x 69" piece of batting

Cutting
From the blue tone-on-tone fabric, cut:
- 12 strips, 2½" x 42"

From the green tone-on-tone fabric, cut:
- 12 strips, 2½" x 42"

From the white solid, cut:
- 9 strips, 4½" x 42"
- 9 strips, 6" x 42"; crosscut into 49 squares, 6" x 6"

Constructing the Blocks

1. With right sides together, sew a green strip to a blue strip. Repeat to make a total of nine strip sets. Open and starch each strip set as described in "Starch for Success" on page 7.

Make 9.

2. Referring to "Cutting Triangles" on page 7, cut six 90° double-strip triangles from each strip set and six solid triangles from each white 4½" x 42" strip. Starch each white triangle to preserve the bias edges.

3. Separate the triangles into three sets:
   - 27 green tip/blue strip
   - 27 blue tip/green strip
   - 54 white solid

Make 27.   Make 27.   Make 54.

Designed by Kathy Brown; pieced by Linda Reed; quilted by Carol Hilton

4. With right sides together, sew a white triangle to each pieced triangle. Starch each block to preserve the bias edges of the triangles.

Make 27. Make 27.

Assembling the Quilt Top

1. Using a design wall or other flat surface, arrange the completed blocks and white 6" squares as shown in the quilt assembly diagram below. (**Note:** You'll have two of each block style left over.)
2. Sew the blocks and squares in each row together; press. Sew the rows together to complete the quilt top; press.

Finishing

Refer to "Completing the Quilt" on page 10 as needed.

1. Layer the quilt top with batting and backing. Baste the layers, and then quilt as desired.
2. Sew the remaining blue and green 2½" x 42" strips together randomly to make one long strip, and use the strip to bind the quilt.

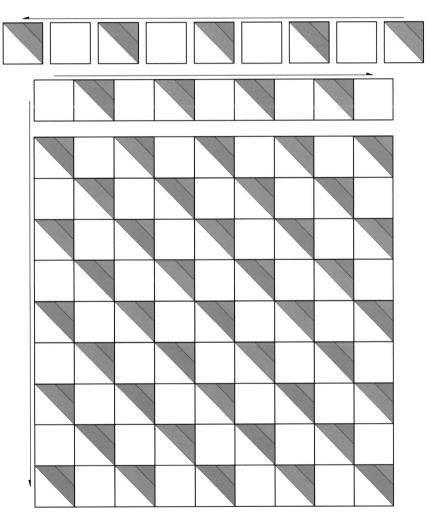

Quilt assembly

Starburst

Finished quilt: 59½" x 59½" ➤ **Finished block:** 5½" x 5½"

Star blocks are among my favorite quilt blocks—in large part because they can be designed and made in such a wide variety of ways. As I was working with strip sets for this book, I thought it would be wonderful to come up with a center Star block that seemed to burst from the quilt in all directions. As stubborn and determined as I can be when I set my mind to something, I knew this quilt would eventually become a reality—and it did. In all its glory, here is "Starburst" for you to make and enjoy as much as I have!

Materials
Yardage is based on 42"-wide fabric.
4 yards of cream print for block, borders, and binding
1 yard of red print for blocks
1 yard of green print for blocks
4½ yards of fabric for backing
68" x 68" piece of batting

Cutting
From the red print, cut:
- 11 strips, 2½" x 42"

From the green print, cut:
- 11 strips, 2" x 42"

From the cream print, cut:
- 10 strips, 4½" x 42"
- 7 strips, 2½" x 42"
- 3 strips, 6" x 42"; crosscut into 16 squares, 6" x 6"
- 2 strips, 3" x 22½"
- 2 strips, 3" x 27½"
- 2 strips, 3" x 38½"
- 4 strips, 3" x 24"
- 8 strips, 3" x 34"

Constructing the Blocks
1. With right sides together, sew a green strip to a red strip. Repeat to make a total of 11 strip sets. Open and starch each strip set as described in "Starch for Success" on page 7.

Make 11.

2. Referring to "Cutting Triangles" on page 7, cut six 90° double-strip triangles from each strip set and six solid triangles from each cream 4½" x 42" strip. Starch each cream triangle to preserve the bias edges.
3. Separate the triangles into three sets. (**Note:** You'll have two cream triangles left over.)
   - 33 green tip/red strip
   - 33 red tip/green strip
   - 58 cream solid

Make 33.   Make 33.   Make 58.

4. With right sides together, join a green tip/red strip triangle and a red tip/green strip triangle as shown. Repeat to make a total of four blocks. Starch each block to preserve the bias edges of the triangles.

Make 4.

Designed by Kathy Brown; pieced by Linda Reed; quilted by Carol Hilton

5. With right sides together, sew a cream triangle to each of the remaining green tip/red strip and red tip/green strip triangles as shown. Starch each block to preserve the bias edges of the triangles.

Make 29. Make 29.

Assembling the Quilt Top

1. Using a design wall or other flat surface, arrange the blocks and cream 6" squares into four horizontal rows as shown. Sew the blocks and squares in each row together; press. Sew the rows together to complete the center star unit; press.

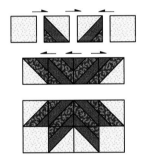 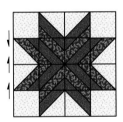

2. Sew the cream 3" x 22½" strips to the sides of the center star unit. Press the seam allowances toward the border strips. Sew the cream 3" x 27½" strips to the top and bottom of the center star unit. Press the seam allowances toward the border strips.

3. Arrange the blocks and cream 6" squares around the center unit as shown. Sew the blocks on each side together; press. Sew these strips to the sides of the quilt top; press. Sew the blocks along the top and bottom together;

press. Sew these strips to the top and bottom of the quilt top; press.

4. Sew the cream 3" x 38½" strips to the sides of the quilt top; press the seam allowances toward the border strips. Sew two cream 3" x 24" strips together end to end to make one long strip. Repeat to make a second pieced strip. Trim each pieced strip to 43½" long, and sew these strips to the top and bottom of the quilt top. Press the seam allowances toward the border strips.

5. Repeat step 3 to arrange the blocks and squares around the quilt center as shown. Join the blocks and then sew the borders to the quilt center.

6. Referring to "Adding Borders" on page 10, join two cream 3" x 34" strips to make one long strip. Repeat to make a total of four pieced strips. Sew the strips to the quilt top for the outer border; press and trim.

Finishing

Refer to "Completing the Quilt" on page 10 as needed.

1. Layer the quilt top with batting and backing. Baste the layers, and then quilt as desired.
2. Sew the cream 2½" x 42" strips together to make one long strip, and use the strip to bind the quilt.

Quilt assembly

Bull's-Eye

When I was in middle school (or junior high as we called it), we had physical education class every day. While the boys were outside playing flag football, baseball, basketball, and other sports, the girls were indoors learning dancing and other "fun" activities. Being a total tomboy, I was bored to tears and wishing that I was outside with the boys. Then one day fate intervened, and the school administration decided to put our formerly segregated PE classes together into one big, happy family—boys and girls together. We were all going to learn the sport of archery, and I couldn't have been more thrilled! What started out as a two-week rotation in PE class turned into a sport that I absolutely loved, discovered I was good at, and ended up practicing for many years to come! The blocks formed in this strip-smart quilt remind me of those practice targets I used to take aim for, so I promptly named this fun quilt "Bull's-Eye."

Materials

Yardage is based on 42"-wide fabric.

2⅛ yards of large-scale brown floral for outer border and binding

2 yards of red floral for blocks and middle border

1¾ yards of cream floral for blocks and inner border

1⅝ yards of small-scale brown floral for blocks

5½ yards of fabric for backing

75" x 92" piece of batting

Cutting

From the small-scale brown floral, cut:
- 8 strips, 2½" x 42"
- 8 strips, 3¼" x 42"
- 6 squares, 6" x 6"

From the red floral, cut:
- 8 strips, 1½" x 42"
- 8 strips, 2½" x 42"
- 8 strips, 3¼" x 42"
- 6 squares, 6" x 6"

From the cream floral, cut:
- 8 strips, 4½" x 42"
- 8 strips, 2½" x 42"

From the large-scale brown floral, cut:
- 8 strips, 6" x 42"
- 8 strips, 2½" x 42"

Constructing the Blocks

1. With right sides together, sew a small-scale brown floral 2½" x 42" strip to a red floral 2½" x 42" strip. Repeat to make a total of eight brown/red strip sets. Open and starch each strip set as described in "Starch for Success" on page 7.

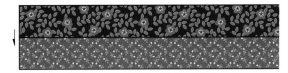

Make 8.

2. Referring to "Cutting Triangles" on page 7, cut six 90° double-strip triangles from each strip set and six solid triangles from each cream floral 4½" x 42" strip. Starch each cream triangle to preserve the bias edges.

3. Separate the triangles into three sets:
   - 24 red tip/brown strip
   - 24 brown tip/red strip
   - 48 cream solid

Make 24.   Make 24.   Make 48.

4. With right sides together, sew a cream triangle to each pieced triangle. Starch each block to preserve the bias edges of the triangles.

Make 24.   Make 24.

5. With right sides together, sew a small-scale brown floral 3¼" x 42" strip to a red floral 3¼" x 42" strip; press. Repeat to make a total of eight strip sets. Crosscut the strip sets into 48 segments, 6" wide.

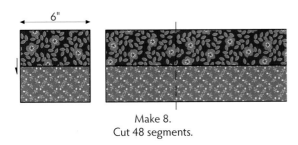

Make 8.
Cut 48 segments.

6. Arrange four red tip/brown strip blocks from step 4, four segments from step 5, and one small-scale brown floral 6" square into three horizontal rows as shown. Sew the pieces in each row together; press. Sew the rows together; press. Repeat to make a total of six brown blocks.

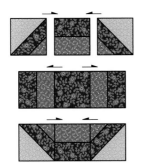 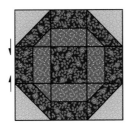

Make 6.

7. Arrange four brown tip/red strip blocks from step 4, four segments from step 5, and one red floral 6" square into three horizontal rows as shown. Sew the pieces in each row together; press. Sew the rows together; press. Repeat to make a total of six red blocks.

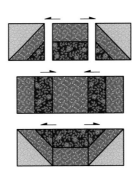 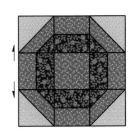

Make 6.

Assembling the Quilt Top

1. Using a design wall or other flat surface, arrange the completed blocks as shown in the quilt assembly diagram on page 45, alternating the brown and red blocks in each row and from row to row.
2. Sew the blocks in each row together; press. Sew the rows together; press.
3. Referring to "Adding Borders" on page 10, join two cream floral 2½" x 42" strips to make one long strip. Repeat to make a total of four pieced strips. Sew the strips to the quilt top for the inner border; press.

Designed by Kathy Brown; pieced by Linda Reed; quilted by Carol Hilton

4. Repeat step 3 to add the red floral 1½"-wide middle-border strips to the quilt top, followed by the large-scale brown floral 6"-wide outer-border strips.

Finishing

Refer to "Completing the Quilt" on page 10 as needed.

1. Layer the quilt top with batting and backing. Baste the layers, and then quilt as desired.
2. Sew the large-scale brown floral 2½" x 42" strips together to make one long strip, and use the strip to bind the quilt.

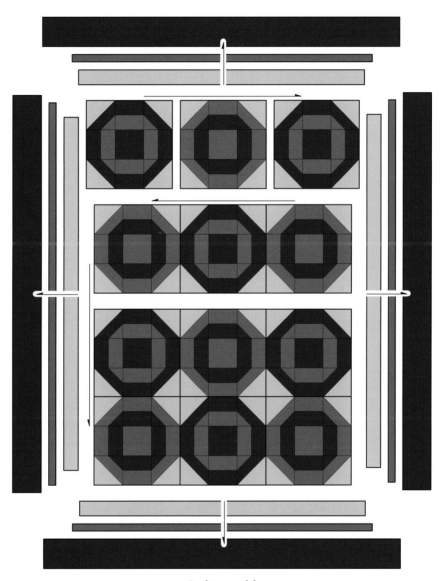

Quilt assembly

Flip-Flops

 As anyone who knows me well can attest, I own so many pairs of flip-flops that I can't even begin to count them. With feet as skinny as skis, and heels that are even narrower, I have a terrible time finding regular shoes that fit, let alone fit well! I quickly found out that flip-flops suit my feet just fine. Allowing the open air to circulate and with nothing to slip off my heel, flip-flops are the perfect alternative to shoes that hurt and are a constant bother. Add today's trendy styles to the mix, and I'm one flip-flop-wearing, happy kind of girl! I guess it's a good thing I live in the Deep South and can wear them year-round, right?

As I placed the blocks in this quilt on my design wall, they instantly reminded me of my closet full of brightly colored footwear. And a simple turning of the block upward or downward—flipped and flopped—inspired the perfectly apt name for this fun quilt. Why not grab a stash of strips and start your own version of "Flip-Flops"?

Materials

Yardage is based on 42"-wide fabric.

3½ yards of white solid for blocks

34 assorted 2½" x 42" strips for blocks and binding

3⅞ yards of fabric for backing

63" x 80" piece of batting

Cutting

From the white solid, cut:

- 11 strips, 4½" x 42"
- 32 rectangles, 6" x 11½"

From *each* of the 2½" x 42" strips, cut:

- 1 strip, 2½" x 30"; reserve the remainder of the strip for the binding (34 total)

Constructing the Blocks

1. With right sides together, join two assorted 2½" x 30" strips. Repeat to make a total of 17 strip sets. Open and starch each strip set as described in "Starch for Success" on page 7.

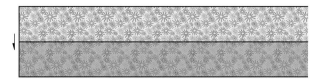

Make 17 assorted.

2. Referring to "Cutting Triangles" on page 7, cut four 90° double-strip triangles from each strip set and six solid triangles from each white 4½" x 42" strip. Starch each white triangle to preserve the bias edges.

Make 34.   Make 34.   Make 66.

3. With right sides together, sew each white triangle to a pieced triangle to make 33 matching pairs. (**Note:** You'll have one pair of matching triangles left over.) Starch each square to preserve the bias edges of the triangles.

Make 33 matching pairs total.

Designed by Kathy Brown; pieced by Linda Reed; quilted by Carol Hilton

4. Sew two matching squares together as shown. Press the seam allowances in either direction. Repeat to make a total of 33 blocks.

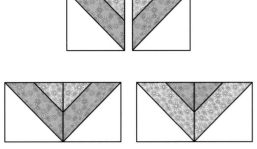

Make 33 total.

Assembling the Quilt Top

1. Using a design wall or other flat surface, arrange the blocks and white 6" x 11½" rectangles into rows as shown in the quilt assembly diagram below.

2. Sew the blocks and rectangles in each row together; press. Sew the rows together; press.

Finishing

Refer to "Completing the Quilt" on page 10 as needed.

1. Layer the quilt top with batting and backing. Baste the layers, and then quilt as desired.

2. Sew the reserved 2½"-wide strips together randomly to make one long strip, and use the strip to bind the quilt.

Quilt assembly

Calm before the Storm

Finished quilt: 58½" x 73½" ➤ **Finished block:** 13" x 13"

I love the rain on a cold, dreary day. Cuddled up inside my home, safe and warm, I love to watch as the sky turns gray and the light outside gives way to that yellow cast that lasts for only a few moments before the rain begins to fall. As the rain comes down, I get a sense of pleasure knowing that the earth is cleansing itself and will start anew once the storm has passed. It's those few moments captured in time that this quilt reminded me of with its yellow and gray palette—soft and gentle, like a winter's rain.

Materials

Yardage is based on 42"-wide fabric.
2½ yards of cream print for blocks and
    sashing strips
2¼ yards of yellow print for blocks and border
1⅜ yards of gray print for blocks, sashing corner-
    stones, and binding
4⅛ yards of fabric for backing
66" x 81" piece of batting

Cutting

From the yellow print, cut:
- 8 strips, 6" x 42"
- 8 strips, 2½" x 42"
- 6 squares, 2½" x 2½"

From the gray print, cut:
- 18 strips, 2½" x 42"; crosscut *2 of the strips* into
  26 squares, 2½" x 2½"

From the cream print, cut:
- 18 strips, 2½" x 42"; crosscut into:
  31 strips, 2½" x 13½"
  48 rectangles, 2½" x 6"
- 8 strips, 4½" x 42"

Constructing the Blocks

1. With right sides together, sew a yellow
   2½" x 42" strip to a gray 2½" x 42" strip. Repeat
   to make a total of eight strip sets. Open and
   starch each strip set as described in "Starch for Success" on page 7.

Make 8.

2. Referring to "Cutting Triangles" on page 7, cut six 90° double-strip triangles from each strip set and six solid triangles from each cream 4½" x 42" strip. Starch each cream triangle to preserve the bias edges.

3. Separate the triangles into three sets:
   - 24 yellow tip/gray strip
   - 24 gray tip/yellow strip
   - 48 cream solid

Make 24.   Make 24.   Make 48.

4. With right sides together, sew a cream triangle to each pieced triangle as shown. Starch each square to preserve the bias edges.

Make 24.   Make 24.

Designed by Kathy Brown; pieced by Linda Reed; quilted by Carol Hilton

5. Arrange four yellow tip/gray strip squares from step 4, four cream 2½" x 6" rectangles, and one gray 2½" square into three horizontal rows as shown. Sew the pieces in each row together; press. Sew the rows together; press. Repeat to make a total of six blocks.

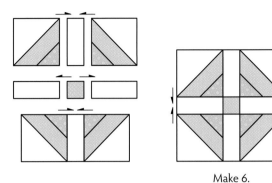

Make 6.

6. Arrange four gray tip/yellow strip squares from step 4, four cream 2½" x 6" rectangles, and one yellow 2½" square into three horizontal rows as shown. Sew the pieces in each row together; press. Sew the rows together; press. Repeat to make a total of six blocks.

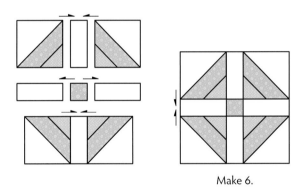

Make 6.

Assembling the Quilt Top

1. Using a design wall or other flat surface, arrange the blocks, cream 2½" x 13½" sashing strips, and gray 2½" cornerstones as shown in the quilt assembly diagram above right.
2. Sew the cornerstones and sashing strips together in each sashing row; press.
3. Sew the sashing strips and blocks together in each block row; press.

4. Sew the rows together to form the quilt top; press.
5. Referring to "Adding Borders" on page 10, join two yellow 6" x 42" strips to make one long strip. Repeat to make a total of four pieced strips. Sew the border strips to the quilt top; press and trim.

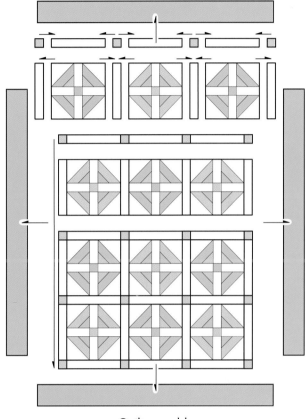

Quilt assembly

Finishing

Refer to "Completing the Quilt" on page 10 as needed.

1. Layer the quilt top with batting and backing. Baste the layers, and then quilt as desired.
2. Sew the remaining gray 2½" x 42" strips together to make one long strip, and use the strip to bind the quilt.

The Mall

Our family is big on traditions, and one of our favorites is to head to the mall the day after Thanksgiving—along with a million other frantic Christmas shoppers. The sights and sounds and fun of it all were a delight to our young daughter, and my husband took each foray into the masses in stride. As the years passed, the trips became a little bit harder for "good-old dad" to endure. Waiting in endless lines at the registers made him long for the comforts of home away from the craziness!

One year he announced he was heading to the center of the mall to wait. As my daughter and I stared at him in confusion, he explained that the center was the best spot to be, because no matter which direction you turned, you were facing a way out! These days when my daughter and I make our annual trek to the mall, sometimes, just sometimes, you can find her dad in the center of the mall, waiting as patiently as ever.

Setting the blocks as shown depicts the center of the mall—with all the other blocks pointing outward. Honey, this quilt's for you!

Materials
Yardage is based on 42"-wide fabric.
3½ yards of navy print for blocks and outer border
18 assorted medium-value print 2½" x 42" strips for blocks and inner border
17 assorted light-value print 2½" x 42" strips for blocks and inner border
8 assorted navy print 2½" x 42" strips for binding
4 yards of fabric for backing
67" x 78" piece of batting

Cutting
From the navy print for blocks and border, cut:
- 14 strips, 4½" x 42"
- 8 strips, 6" x 42"

Constructing the Blocks
1. With right sides together, sew a light print strip to a medium print strip. Repeat to make a total of 14 strip sets. Open and starch each strip set as described in "Starch for Success" on page 7.

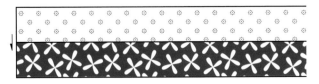

Make 14 assorted.

2. Referring to "Cutting Triangles" on page 7, cut six 90° double-strip triangles from each strip set and six solid triangles from each navy 4½" x 42" strip. Starch each navy triangle to preserve the bias edges.

Make 84.   Make 84.

3. With right sides together, sew each navy triangle to a pieced triangle. Starch each square to preserve the bias edges of the triangles.

Make 84.

4. With right sides together, join two squares from step 3 as shown on page 57. Repeat to make a total of 42 blocks. Wait to press the block seam allowances until you've arranged the quilt top for assembly. (**Note:** You'll have

Designed by Kathy Brown; pieced by Linda Reed; quilted by Carol Hilton

two blocks left over, giving you added variety when laying out the quilt.)

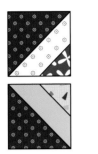

Make 42.

Assembling the Quilt Top

1. Using a design wall or other flat surface, arrange 40 of the blocks as shown in the quilt assembly diagram below. Press the block seam allowances in alternate directions so they'll oppose each other when sewn together.
2. Sew the blocks in each row together; press. Sew the rows together; press.

3. Cut each of the remaining seven assorted print strips into two random-length pieces. Sew the strips together using a diagonal seam to make one long strip. Referring to "Adding Borders" on page 10, use the pieced strip to sew the inner border to the quilt top; press and trim.
4. Referring to "Adding Borders," join two navy 6" x 42" strips to make one long strip. Repeat to make a total of four pieced strips. Sew the strips to the quilt top for the outer border; press and trim.

Finishing

Refer to "Completing the Quilt" on page 10 as needed.

1. Layer the quilt top with batting and backing. Baste the layers, and then quilt as desired.
2. Sew the assorted navy 2½" x 42" strips together to make one long strip, and use the strip to bind the quilt.

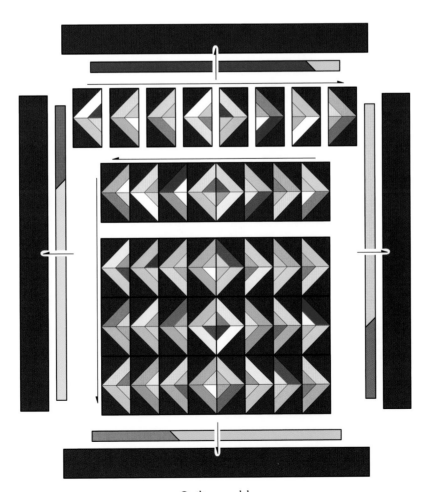

Quilt assembly

Kissy Fishy

Finished quilt: 64½" x 80½" ➤ **Finished block:** 8" x 8"

Sometimes a quilt comes together, well, just because—because I liked the fabric, or because I got a wild hair, or because I wanted to clean out my stash, or because of any of a hundred other reasons! In this case, I had been gathering a bunch of batik fabrics and wanted to use them in a very scrappy way. I knew they would all have to play together well, so I made sure I stuck to bright color families. But other than that, anything I gathered was OK! I cut the fabrics into 2½"-wide strips, set them aside, and waited for the day that I'd be ready to put them all together. That day came when I was playing around with pairs of strip-smart triangles, and the resulting block looked like two kissing fish. Voilà—"Kissy Fishy" was born!

Although I used batiks in this quilt, any fabrics in any print would work well. Just make sure your color families play nicely together as mine did, and you'll be on your way to making your very own version of "Kissy Fishy" in no time at all.

Materials

Yardage is based on 42"-wide fabric.

4 yards of white tone-on-tone fabric for blocks and border

52 assorted bright batik 2½" x 42" strips for blocks and binding

5 yards of fabric for backing

72" x 88" piece of batting

Cutting

From the white tone-on-tone fabric, cut:
- 29 strips, 4½" x 42"

From *each of 10* of the assorted bright batik strips, cut:
- 3 strips, 2½" x 11" (30 total)

Constructing the Blocks

1. With right sides together, join two different-colored batik 2½" x 42" strips to make a strip set. Repeat to make a total of 21 strip sets. Open and starch the strip sets as described in "Starch for Success" on page 7.

Make 21 assorted.

2. Referring to "Cutting Triangles" on page 7, cut six 90° double-strip triangles from each strip set and six solid triangles from each of 21 of the white tone-on-tone 4½" x 42" strips. Starch each white triangle to preserve the bias edges.

Make 63.

Make 63.

Make 126.

Designed by Kathy Brown; pieced by Linda Reed; quilted by Carol Hilton

3. Select two triangles from the same strip set but with the fabrics in opposite positions. Sew each triangle to a white triangle as shown; press. Sew the triangle pairs together to complete the block. Repeat to make a total of 63 blocks. Starch each block to preserve the bias edges of the triangles.

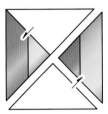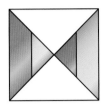

Make 63 assorted.

Assembling the Quilt Top

1. Using a design wall or other flat surface, arrange the completed blocks as shown in the quilt assembly diagram below.
2. Sew the blocks in each row together; press. Sew the rows together; press.
3. Referring to "Adding Borders" on page 10, join two of the remaining white 4½" x 42" strips to make one long strip. Repeat to make a total of four pieced strips. Sew the border strips to the quilt top; press and trim.

Finishing

Refer to "Completing the Quilt" on page 10 as needed.

1. Layer the quilt top with batting and backing. Baste the layers, and then quilt as desired.
2. Sew the assorted batik 2½" x 11" strips together randomly to make one long strip, and use the strip to bind the quilt.

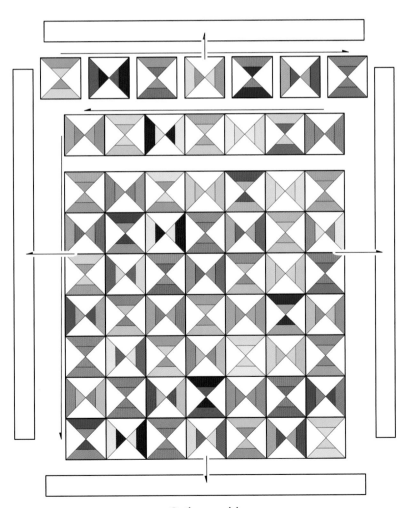

Quilt assembly ◄

Flying South

Finished quilt: 54½" x 70½" ➤ **Finished block:** 11" x 11"

As a child I'd spend many afternoons lying on the ground, looking up at the sky and imagining all kinds of wondrous things that the clouds represented. One of my favorite daydreaming spots was across the street from my childhood home, where there stood, tall and proud, the biggest oak tree you can imagine. On crisp, cool autumn days, I loved to lie cradled in the roots of that tree and stare up at the skies dreaming of any number of things. At times I'd be treated to the sight of a flock of birds flying in V formation as they headed our way for the winter. I still live in the same town where I grew up, so I still see that old oak tree with its majestic roots and gather its acorns to use in my fall decorating. And every once in a while, I glimpse a flock of birds flying in V formation as they head our way for the winter.

I designed this quilt to capture my memories of that special spot and those crisp, cool autumn afternoons. The blue, brown, and cream color scheme represents my old oak tree, the patches of sky that peeked through its branches, and the clouds that inspired so many daydreams.

Materials
Yardage is based on 42"-wide fabric.
3⅞ yards of cream print for blocks, sashing, border, and binding
1⅓ yards of blue print for blocks
1⅓ yards of brown print for blocks
3⅞ yards of fabric for backing
62" x 78" piece of batting

Cutting
From the blue print, cut:
- 16 strips, 2½" x 42"

From the brown print, cut:
- 16 strips, 2½" x 42"

From the cream print, cut:
- 16 strips, 4½" x 42"
- 21 strips, 2½" x 42"

Constructing the Blocks
1. With right sides together, sew a blue strip to a brown strip. Repeat to make a total of 16 strip sets. Open and starch each strip set as described in "Starch for Success" on page 7.

Make 16.

2. Referring to "Cutting Triangles" on page 7, cut six 90° double-strip triangles from each strip set and six solid triangles from each cream 4½" x 42" strip. Starch each cream triangle to preserve the bias edges.
3. Separate the triangles into three sets:
   - 48 blue tip/brown strip
   - 48 brown tip/blue strip
   - 96 cream solid

Make 48.   Make 48.   Make 96.

Designed by Kathy Brown; pieced by Linda Reed; quilted by Carol Hilton

4. With right sides together, sew a cream triangle to each pieced triangle as shown. Starch each square to preserve the bias edges of the triangles.

Make 48. Make 48.

5. With right sides together, sew a blue tip/brown strip square to a brown tip/blue strip square as shown, orienting them so that a strip forms from the top left to the bottom right. Repeat to make a total of 24 units; press.

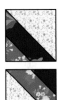 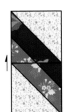

Make 24.

6. Repeat step 5 to make 24 units with the remaining squares from step 4, orienting them so that a strip forms from the bottom left to the top right.

 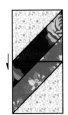

Make 24.

7. Sew each unit from step 5 to a unit from step 6 as shown. Press the seam allowances of half of the units in one direction and the remaining half in the opposite direction.

Make 24.

Assembling the Quilt Top

1. Using a design wall or other flat surface, arrange the completed blocks in vertical rows as shown in the quilt assembly diagram below, alternating the pressing direction of each block so the seam allowances will nest together.
2. Sew the blocks in each row together; press.
3. Referring to "Adding Borders" on page 10, join two cream 2½" x 42" strips to make one long strip. Repeat to make a total of seven pieced strips. Sew a pieced strip between each block row for the sashing; press and trim. Sew the remaining pieced strips to the quilt top for the border; press and trim.

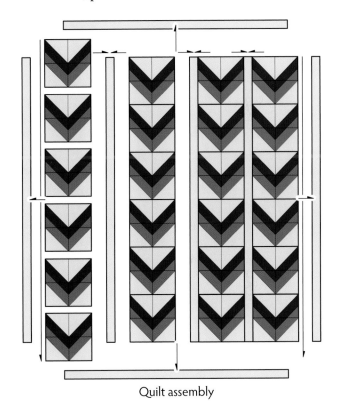

Quilt assembly

Finishing

Refer to "Completing the Quilt" on page 10 as needed.

1. Layer the quilt top with batting and backing. Baste the layers, and then quilt as desired.
2. Sew the remaining cream 2½" x 42" strips together to make one long strip, and use the strip to bind the quilt.

Don't Beat around the Bush

Finished table runner: 24" x 70½" ➤ **Finished block:** 16½" x 16½"

Being raised as a proper Southern gal in the late 1950s and early '60s, I was taught to be many things—but never, ever was I allowed to be mean spirited. I could think what I wanted, have my own opinions about anything, but when it came to expressing those opinions, I'd better say something nice and with grace if I was going to open my mouth and express anything at all! To this day, expressing my true feelings if I don't care for something is very hard for me. I tend to act neutral and "beat around the bush." When I chose the fabrics for this table runner, they reminded me of that phrase. The golds and reds are my true Southern side served with a dash of grace, while the black is my inner voice just begging to pipe up and state what I truly feel from time to time. What colors will you choose if you decide to "beat around the bush"?

Materials

Yardage is based on 42"-wide fabric.

2⅜ yards of gold print for blocks, setting triangles, and binding

⅓ yard of red print for blocks

⅓ yard of black print for blocks

2 yards of fabric for backing

32" x 78" piece of batting

Cutting

From the red print, cut:
- 2 strips, 2½" x 42"
- 6 squares, 3" x 3"

From the black print, cut:
- 2 strips, 2½" x 42"
- 6 squares, 3" x 3"

From the gold print, cut:
- 3 strips, 6" x 42"; crosscut into 15 squares, 6" x 6"
- 2 strips, 4½" x 42"
- 5 strips, 2½" x 42"
- 1 square, 24½" x 24½"; cut into quarters diagonally to yield 4 side setting triangles
- 2 squares, 12½" x 12½"; cut in half diagonally to yield 4 corner setting triangles

Constructing the Blocks

1. With right sides together, sew a red strip to a black strip. Repeat to make a second strip set. Open and starch the strip sets as described in "Starch for Success" on page 7.

Make 2.

2. Referring to "Cutting Triangles" on page 7, cut six 90° double-strip triangles from each strip set and six solid triangles from each gold 4½" x 42" strip. Starch each gold triangle to preserve the bias edges.

3. Separate the triangles into three sets:
   - 6 red tip/black strip
   - 6 black tip/red strip
   - 12 gold solid

Make 6.   Make 6.   Make 12.

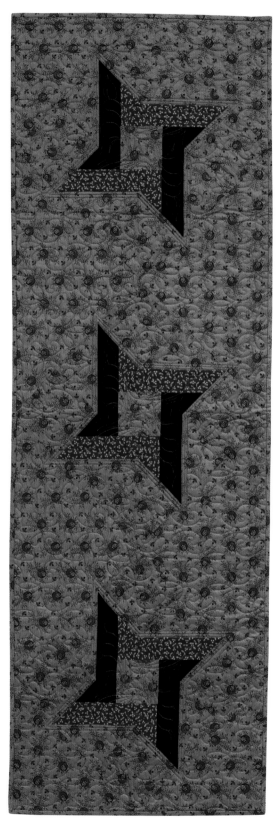

Designed by Kathy Brown; pieced by Linda Reed; quilted by Carol Hilton

4. With right sides together, sew a gold triangle to each pieced triangle as shown. Starch each square to preserve the bias edges of the triangles.

Make 6.   Make 6.

5. Draw a diagonal line on the wrong side of each red and black 3" square.

6. Position two marked red squares on opposite corners of a gold 6" square, right sides together. Sew on the marked lines. Trim ¼" from the stitching lines. Press the red triangles toward the corners. Repeat on the remaining two corners of the gold square using two marked black squares. Repeat to make a total of three center squares.

Make 3.

7. Arrange two red tip/black strip squares and two black tip/red strip squares from step 4, one center square from step 6, and four gold 6" squares into three horizontal rows as shown. Sew the squares in each row together; press. Sew the rows together; press. Repeat to make a total of three blocks.

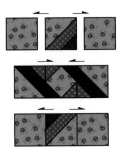 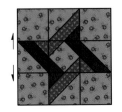

Make 3.

Assembling the Table-Runner Top

1. Using a design wall or other flat surface, arrange the completed blocks and the gold side and corner setting triangles into diagonal rows as shown in the assembly diagram below.

2. Sew the block and setting triangles in each row together; press. Sew the rows together; press. Add the remaining corner triangles; press.

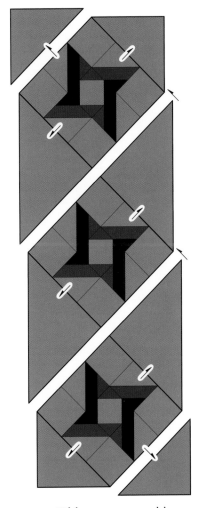

Table-runner assembly

Finishing

Refer to "Completing the Quilt" on page 10 as needed.

1. Layer the table-runner top with batting and backing. Baste the layers, and then quilt as desired.

2. Sew the gold 2½" x 42" strips together to make one long strip, and use the strip to bind the table runner.

In Honor

"In Honor": In honor of all the brave men and women of our past who fought for our freedoms. In honor of all the brave men and women of today who take on this task with pride. In honor of all the brave men and women yet to come who will follow in their footsteps. I honor you and thank you for your service, your commitment, your dedication, your sacrifice, and your courage. You are the true heroes of our great nation.

Materials
Yardage is based on 42"-wide fabric.
2 yards of white tone-on-tone fabric for blocks
1⅔ yards of red print for blocks
1¼ yards of navy print for flag canton and binding
2⅞ yards of fabric for backing
47" x 69" piece of batting

Cutting
From the red print, cut:
- 21 strips, 2½" x 42"

From the white tone-on-tone fabric, cut:
- 21 strips, 2½" x 42"
- 2 strips, 4½" x 42"

From the navy print, cut:
- 1 square, 22½" x 22½"
- 6 strips, 2½" x 42"

Constructing the Blocks
1. With right sides together, sew a white strip to a red strip. Repeat to make a total of 21 strip sets. Open and starch each strip set as described in "Starch for Success" on page 7.

Make 21.

2. Referring to "Cutting Triangles" on page 7, cut six 90° double-strip triangles from each strip set and six solid triangles from each white tone-on-tone 4½" x 42" strip. Starch each white triangle to preserve the bias edges.

3. Separate the triangles into three sets. (**Note:** You'll have two white tip/red strip triangles, nine red tip/white strip triangles, and five white tone-on-tone triangles left over.)
   - 61 white tip/red strip
   - 54 red tip/white strip
   - 7 white solid

Make 61.   Make 54.   Make 7.

4. With right sides together, sew a white tip/red strip triangle to a red tip/white strip triangle as shown to make block A. Repeat to make a total of 54 blocks. Starch each block to preserve the bias edges of the triangles.

Block A.
Make 54.

Designed by Kathy Brown; pieced by Linda Reed; quilted by Carol Hilton

5. With right sides together, sew a white tip/red strip triangle to a white solid triangle as shown to make block B. Repeat to make a total of seven blocks. Starch each block to preserve the bias edges.

Block B.
Make 7.

Assembling the Quilt Top

1. Using a design wall or other flat surface, arrange the completed blocks in two sections as shown in the quilt assembly diagram below. Use the B blocks in the top row of the upper section.

2. Sew the blocks in each row of the upper section together; press. Sew these rows together; press. Join the navy square to the left edge of this section; press.

3. Sew the blocks in each row of the lower section together; press. Sew these rows together. Join this section to the bottom edge of the upper section; press.

Finishing

Refer to "Completing the Quilt" on page 10 as needed.

1. Layer the quilt top with batting and backing. Baste the layers, and then quilt as desired.

2. Sew the navy 2½" x 42" strips together to make one long strip, and use the strip to bind the quilt.

Quilt assembly

Crow's Feet

Several years ago I developed the idea of creating bed runners—small quilts for the foot of the bed to keep your toes toasty on cool nights when a full quilt is just a tad too much warmth! A bed runner also functions as a decorative accent to any bedroom, be it a college dorm room, kid's bedroom, guest room, or master bedroom. So quick to make and so versatile, bed runners allow you to change the look of a bedroom quickly for any occasion at all.

With this bed runner, I think I've got a match made in heaven. Turn some strip-smart blocks into stars with crow's-feet edges, and then stitch them into a small quilt. Indeed, it's a winner of a bed runner!

Materials

Yardage is based on 42"-wide fabric.

1½ yards of white print for blocks, sashing strips, and inner border

1⅜ yards of red print for blocks, middle border, and binding

1⅛ yards of gray print for blocks and outer border

2⅔ yards of fabric for backing

39" x 85" piece of batting

Cutting

From the red print, cut:
- 12 strips, 2½" x 42"
- 6 strips, 1½" x 42"
- 4 squares, 6" x 6"
- 2 squares, 1½" x 1½"

From the gray print, cut:
- 12 strips, 2½" x 42"
- 1 square, 1½" x 1½"
- 8 squares, 6" x 6"

From the white print, cut:
- 2 strips, 6" x 42"; crosscut into 12 squares, 6" x 6"
- 4 strips, 4½" x 42"
- 12 strips, 1½" x 42"; crosscut 6 *of the strips* into:
  2 strips, 1½" x 23½"
  12 strips, 1½" x 11½"

Constructing the Blocks

1. With right sides together, sew a red 2½" x 42" strip to a gray 2½" x 42" strip. Repeat to make a total of six strip sets.

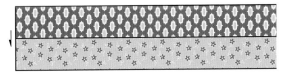

Make 6.

2. Referring to "Cutting Triangles" on page 7, cut six 90° double-strip triangles from each strip set and six solid triangles from each white 4½" x 42" strip. Starch each white triangle to preserve the bias edges.

3. Separate the triangles into three sets. (**Note:** You'll have 10 red tip/gray strip triangles and two gray tip/red strip triangles left over.)
   - 8 red tip/gray strip
   - 16 gray tip/red strip
   - 24 white solid

Make 8.   Make 16.   Make 24.

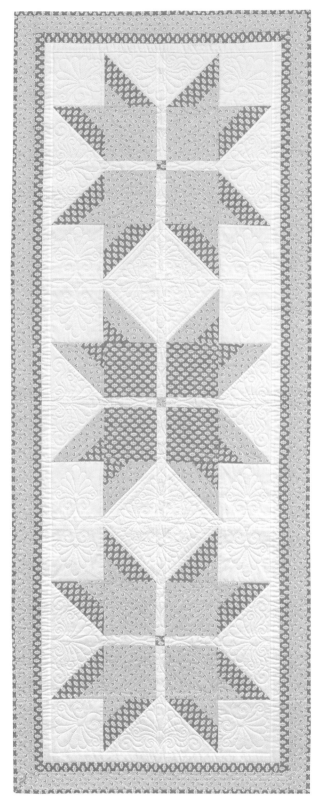

Designed by Kathy Brown; pieced by Linda Reed; quilted by Carol Hilton

4. With right sides together, sew a white triangle to each pieced triangle as shown. Starch each square to preserve the bias edges of the triangles.

Make 8.   Make 16.

5. To make the center block, sew each of four red tip/gray strip squares from step 4 to a white 6" square. Make two of each unit as shown; press.

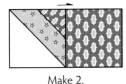 

Make 2.   Make 2.

6. Sew each of the remaining four red tip/gray strip squares from step 4 to a red 6" square. Make two of each unit as shown; press.

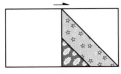 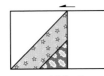

Make 2.   Make 2.

7. Sew the units from steps 5 and 6 together as shown; press.

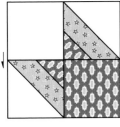 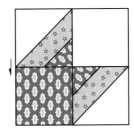

Make 2.   Make 2.

8. Arrange the units from step 7, four white 1½" x 11½" strips, and the gray 1½" square into three horizontal rows as shown for the center block. Sew the pieces in each row together; press. Sew the rows together; press.

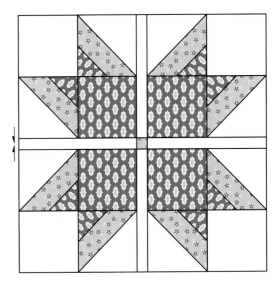

9. To make the end blocks, sew each of eight gray tip/red strip squares from step 4 to a white 6" square. Make four of each unit as shown; press.

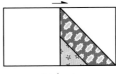 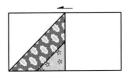

Make 4.   Make 4.

10. Sew each of the remaining eight gray tip/red strip squares from step 4 to a gray 6" square. Make four of each unit as shown; press.

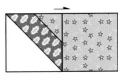 

Make 4.   Make 4.

11. Sew the units from steps 9 and 10 together as shown; press.

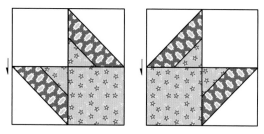

Make 4 of each.

12. Arrange two of each unit from step 11, four white 1½" x 11½" strips, and one red 1½" square into three horizontal rows as shown. Sew the pieces in each row together; press. Sew the rows together; press. Repeat to make a total of two blocks.

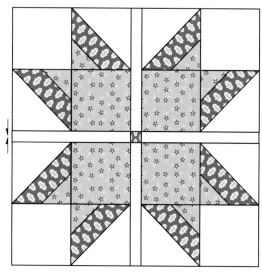

Make 2.

Assembling the Bed-Runner Top

1. Using a design wall or other flat surface, arrange the completed blocks and white 1½" x 23½" sashing strips as shown in the assembly diagram at right.

2. Sew the blocks and sashing strips together to form the quilt top; press.

3. Referring to "Adding Borders" on page 10, join two white 1½" x 42" strips to make one long strip. Repeat to make a second pieced strip. Sew the strips to the long sides of the bed-runner top for the inner border; press and trim. Sew the remaining white 1½" x 42" strips

to the short ends of the bed-runner top; press and trim.

4. Repeat step 3 to add the red 1½"-wide middle-border strips, followed by the gray 2½"-wide outer-border strips.

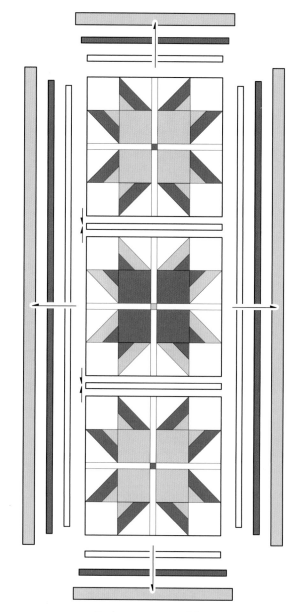

Bed-runner assembly

Finishing

Refer to "Completing the Quilt" on page 10 as needed.

1. Layer the quilt top with batting and backing. Baste the layers, and then quilt as desired.

2. Sew the red 2½" x 42" strips together to make one long strip, and use the strip to bind the quilt.

Acknowledgments

With a grateful heart, I give warm thanks to:

My husband, for everything from folding patterns to cleaning house, cooking dinner, and supporting me in whatever else was needed, as always!

My daughter, just for being the light and love of my heart!

Linda Reed, for being my "everything" kind of friend. Somehow you take my scribbles and scrabbles and transform them into the quilts I knew they could be.

Carol Hilton, for her long-arm quilting expertise. My quilts have become known for their beautiful quilting designs and it's all because of your talents. I'm forever grateful to be one of your clients and friends.

Debbie Bamber, for always being there at a moment's notice to add your wonderful binding to these quilts.

Tara Darr, Debbie Field, and Paula Toups—the best of friends, and my true soul sisters through it all! I'm so blessed to have you as my friends.

Red Rooster Fabrics, especially Anna and Carol. You work diligently to bring my fabric ideas into artful elegance, and I am forever honored to be one of your designers.

The quilters who buy my patterns, books, and fabrics: you continue to let me live my dream of loving my work by supporting my efforts.

The quilt shops that buy my patterns, books, and fabrics: for supporting me, teaching classes from my designs, and making quilts with my fabrics. I'm honored that you consider my efforts worthy of your time and patronage.

And last but not least, Karen S., Cathy R., Mary B., Karen B., Mary G., and the rest of the fabulous staff at Martingale for their faith in me once again. You are the best!

About the Author

Nineteen years have passed since I began my quilting journey. What started out as a simple appliquéd sweatshirt has evolved into so much more. Designing my own quilts, rulers for Creative Grids, fabrics for Red Rooster, and quilts for books with Martingale—these things have afforded me a very rewarding work life. Yet as I travel the country lecturing and teaching, I have been blessed to meet the most wonderful people through this quilting journey, and *that* has turned out to be the most rewarding aspect. It's the quilters along the way who have enriched my life and made all of the work so much more meaningful and fulfilling.

I've often said that I'm the luckiest girl in the world. With this job that fulfills me creatively, a family that loves and supports me, my mini zoo of dogs and cats providing unconditional love, and the best of friends surrounding me, I finally realized that I'm not just lucky, I'm very, very blessed. I get to wake each and every day knowing that I'm living my dream of loving my life *and* my work, and who could ask for more than that?